NTV News24 English 2

日テレNews24 Englishで考える日本事情 2

津田晶子
金志佳代子
Kelly MacDonald

EIHŌSHA

Copyright ©日本テレビ放送網株式会社
Used by permission of Nippon Television Network Corporation

All Rights Reserved.
The printing, copying, redistribution, or retransmission of the Material
without permission of EIHŌSHA is prohibited.

はじめに

『NTV News24 English 2(日テレ News24 Englishで考える日本事情2)』は、時事ニュース番組で日本事情を学びながら、英語の四技能を向上させることを目標とした教材です。各ユニットは以下の構成になっています。

I Warm-up Activity
このユニットで学ぶトピックについて考える問題です。
　　＊日本語・英語、どちらでもかまわないので、自由に考えてみましょう。
　　　写真の描写問題です。
　　＊まずは自分で書いてみましょう。書けたら、ペアやグループで確認して、表現をお互いに学ぶとよいでしょう。

II Listening
TOEIC®形式の写真描写問題です。答え合わせをしたら、音読してみましょう。

III Check Your Vocabulary
このユニットで学ぶ語彙について、定義や綴りを学びます。

IV Note-taking
1回目のリスニングです。ノートを取りながら、だいたいの内容をつかんでみましょう。

V Dictation
2回目以降のリスニングでは、細部をしっかり聴き取って、空欄を埋めます。答え合わせをしたら、音読やシャドーイングをし、巻末付録の記録表に記入しておくとよいでしょう。

VI Comprehension Check
本文の内容が把握できているかを確認する問題です。

VII Write/Speak about Yourself
ユニットのテーマについて、自分自身のことを自由に書いたり、話したりすることで、英語による自己表現能力を養うアクティビティーです。

VIII Vocabulary Building
ユニットのテーマに関連する語彙をクロスワードなどで学びます。日本事情を学ぶのに役立つ語彙や、英語の資格試験に頻出の語彙を習得しましょう。

最後に、本書の構想から出版に至るまで、佐々木元氏、下村幸一氏をはじめとして、英宝社の皆様には大変お世話になりました。心より感謝の意を表します。

津田晶子／金志佳代子／ケリー・マクドナルド

CONTENTS

Chapter 1   ANA Debuts Virtual Travel System 6
ANAが遠隔地体験で新事業

Chapter 2   700,000 Japanese Could Suffer Gambling Addiction 10
ギャンブル依存症実態調査

Chapter 3   University Grad Employment Rate Hits All-time High 14
大学生の就職率過去最高に

Chapter 4   First Self-driving Car Trial on Public Roads 18
全国初の実証実験　公道で無人自動運転

Chapter 5   Japan Mulls Congestion Pricing for Kyoto, Kamakura 22
観光地で通行料金徴収検討

Chapter 6   All Aboard the 'Love Train' 26
京急ラブトレイン運行開始

Chapter 7   Seven Eleven Japan to Add Lockers for E-commerce 30
セブン-イレブンがヤマト宅配ロッカーを店舗に

Chapter 8   Kumamoto Castle Repaired in Symbol of Quake Restoration 34
熊本城にしゃちほこ

Chapter 9   Training to Bike 38
JR東日本サイクルトレイン

Chapter 10   Robot Phone Rentals to Start 42
外国人観光客にロボット型のスマートフォン貸与

Chapter 11   Record Minors Fall Victim to Crimes through Social Media 46
SNSが原因で犯罪被害の児童数過去最高

Chapter 12   New App Aims to Cut Food Waste 50
食品廃棄減らすため　IT活用

Chapter 13   Japan High School Girls Least Happy with Body Shape: Survey 54
体型に不満、日本が一番

Chapter 14   Chiba Likely to Make 'Geologic' History 58
地球史にチバニアン

Chapter 15   Japan May Be Allowed to Boost Tuna Catch 62
太平洋クロマグロ枠拡大へ

Chapter 1
ANA Debuts Virtual Travel System

I Warm-up Activity

Where would you like to go for a holiday?

写真を説明する英文（1 sentence）を書いてみましょう。

II Listening

音声を聴き、写真の説明にもっとも近い英文を選びましょう。

Answer ⒶⒷⒸⒹ

III Check Your Vocabulary 🔊 2

A. 左側の単語にもっとも近い意味をもつ表現を右から選びましょう。

1. virtual   (   )   a. to encourage an activity

2. avatar   (   )   b. to take hold of something

3. grab   (   )   c. seen on the Internet or on a computer

4. official   (   )   d. a person who has a position of responsibility

5. spur   (   )   e. a picture of a person that represents you on a computer screen

B. 左側の定義にあてはまるように、空所を埋めてみましょう。

1. 設備   (e＿＿＿ pment)

2. 水族館   (a＿＿＿ rium)

IV Note-taking 🔊 3

本文を聴きながらノートを取りましょう。（英語でも日本語でも構いません）

7

V Dictation

音声を聴き、（　）を埋めましょう。答え合わせをしたら、音読しましょう。

ANA Debuts Virtual Travel System

Japanese (¹　　　) ANA is launching a new virtual travel experience. The firm unveiled its new avatar system at Tokyo's Haneda Airport. Nippon TV's (²　　　) experiences a fish (³　　　) via a robotic hand. She says she can grab a shellfish. The equipment will allow folks to experience an aquarium in (⁴　　　) Okinawa. ANA plans to debut the avatar system at airports and other locations by next (⁵　　　). Officials hope the simulated travel spurs people to get on airplanes and actually visit the destinations.

http://www.ntv.co.jp/englishnews/economy/ana_debuts_virtual_travel_system/

Score	/ 5

VI Comprehension Check

以下の文章を読んで、内容が正しければT、間違っていればFに○をつけなさい。

1. The new system makes it possible to experience virtual reality.　　(T ／ F)

2. Officials hope the virtual travel experience will boost air travel.　　(T ／ F)

VII　Write/Speak about Yourself

Do you like traveling by airplane? Why or why not?

VIII　Vocabulary Building

下の選択肢から英訳を選び、表を完成させましょう。

空港の英単語	
日本語	英　語
搭乗券	1　(　　　　　　　　　　　　　　　　　　)
金属探知機	2　(　　　　　　　　　　　　　　　　　　)
警備	3　(　　　　　　　　　　　　　　　　　　)
免税店	4　(　　　　　　　　　　　　　　　　　　)
見学デッキ	5　(　　　　　　　　　　　　　　　　　　)
客室乗務員	6　(　　　　　　　　　　　　　　　　　　)
機内食	7　(　　　　　　　　　　　　　　　　　　)
飛行機酔い	8　(　　　　　　　　　　　　　　　　　　)
手荷物受取所	9　(　　　　　　　　　　　　　　　　　　)
税関	10　(　　　　　　　　　　　　　　　　　)

flight attendant　　baggage claim　　in-flight meal　　metal detector　　security
observation deck　　boarding pass　　duty-free shop　　customs　　airsickness

Chapter 2

700,000 Japanese Could Suffer Gambling Addiction

I Warm-up Activity

Do you like playing smartphone games and/or video games?

_____

_____

写真を説明する英文 (1 sentence) を書いてみましょう。

_____

_____

II Listening

音声を聴き、写真の説明にもっとも近い英文を選びましょう。

Answer ▶   Ⓓ

Chapter 2

III Check Your Vocabulary 🔊 5

A. 左側の単語にもっとも近い意味をもつ表現を右から選びましょう。

1. addicted （　　）   a. about, approximately

2. survey   （　　）   b. to be very easy to see or notice

3. figure   （　　）   c. a set of questions that you ask people in order to find their opinion

4. roughly （　　）   d. liking something very much and doing it too often

5. stand out（　　）   e. a number that expresses an amount, especially in official documents

B. [　] 内の文字を並べ替えて、左側の日本語と同意の英単語にしてみましょう。

1. 表す・示す   r[e e e n p s r]t   （　　　　　　　　　　　　　　　　　）

2. 人口   p[a i l o o p t u]n   （　　　　　　　　　　　　　　　　　）

IV Note-taking 🔊 6

本文を聴きながらノートを取りましょう。（英語でも日本語でも構いません）

11

V Dictation 6

音声を聴き、(　)を埋めましょう。答え合わせをしたら、音読しましょう。

700,000 Japanese Could Suffer Gambling Addiction

Some 700,000 adults in Japan could be addicted to gambling. The health ministry today issued the results of a new survey. The figure covers the (¹　　) year and represents about 0.8 percent of the adult population. The ministry received roughly 4,700 replies. Pachinko and slot machines are the biggest (²　　) makers. The (³　　) person spends about 515 dollars a month. Japan's gambling addicted population of 3.6 percent over a lifetime stands out over other (⁴　　). The figure for the Netherlands, for example, is 1.9 percent, while (⁵　　) is only 0.2 percent.

http://www.ntv.co.jp/englishnews/society/700000_japanese_could_suffer_gambling_addiction/

Score	/ 5

VI Comprehension Check

以下の文章を読んで、内容が正しければT，間違っていればFに○をつけなさい。

1. The survey shows that 8 out of 10 people are addicted to gambling in Japan.　(T ／ F)

2. The gambling population in Japan is more than that of the Netherlands.　(T ／ F)

VII   Write/Speak about Yourself

Would you like to visit a casino? Why or why not?

VIII   Vocabulary Building

単語を探しましょう。（たて・よこ・ななめ）

国名の英語表記

C	L	G	R	E	E	C	E
E	A	E	L	R	N	C	E
N	O	R	W	A	Y	A	S
E	A	M	Y	B	W	R	P
D	N	A	L	N	I	F	A
E	D	N	A	L	E	R	I
W	U	Y	T	E	E	L	N
S	M	K	I	N	R	Y	W

ITALY

FINLAND

GREECE

GERMANY

NORWAY

IRELAND

SPAIN

UK

SWEDEN

Chapter 3

University Grad Employment Rate Hits All-time High

I Warm-up Activity

What do you want to do after you graduate?

....

....

写真を説明する英文（1 sentence）を書いてみましょう。

....

....

II Listening   🔊 7

音声を聴き、写真の説明にもっとも近い英文を選びましょう。

Answer ▶ Ⓐ Ⓑ Ⓒ Ⓓ

Chapter 3

III Check Your Vocabulary 🔊 8

A. 左側の単語にもっとも近い意味をもつ表現を右から選びましょう。

1. graduate (   )   a. work, especially physical work

2. release   (   )   b. a desire for a particular activity

3. labor   (   )   c. to find new people to work in a company

4. appetite (   )   d. to let the public have news or information

5. recruit   (   )   e. someone who has completed a university degree

B. [ ]内の文字を並べ替えて、左側の日本語と同意の英単語にしてみましょう。

1. 雇用   e[e l m m n o p y]t   (   )

2. 〜に起因すると考える   a[b i r t t t u]e   (   )

IV Note-taking 🔊 9

本文を聴きながらノートを取りましょう。（英語でも日本語でも構いません）

V Dictation

音声を聴き、（　）を埋めましょう。答え合わせをしたら、音読しましょう。

University Grad Employment Rate Hits All-time High

A record-high 98 percent of this spring's (¹   ) graduates have landed (²   ). Japanese government data released (³   ) showed the employment rate rose for the seventh straight year. By (⁴   ), 97.5 percent of men who graduated in (⁵   ) found work and the figure for women was 98.6 percent. The Labor Ministry attributed the increase to the recovering economy and companies' continued appetite for recruiting.

http://www.ntv.co.jp/englishnews/society/university_grad_employment_rate_hits_all-time_high/

Score	/ 5

VI Comprehension Check

以下の文章を読んで、内容が正しければT，間違っていればFに○をつけなさい。

1. Companies are more willing to hire university graduates in recent years.　（ T ／ F ）

2. The Japanese economy has been improving for more than a decade.　（ T ／ F ）

Chapter 3

VII Write/Speak about Yourself

Describe your ideal workplace.

VIII Vocabulary Building

下の選択肢から英訳を選び、表を完成させましょう。

大学に関する英単語	

日本語	英　語
学科	1 （ ）
教授	2 （ ）
専攻	3 （ ）
副専攻	4 （ ）
1年生	freshman/1st year student
2年生	5 （ ）
3年生	6 （ ）
4年生	7 （ ）
卒業生	8 （ ）
単位	9 （ ）
学位	10 （ ）

alumni	credit	professor	major	department
minor	degree	sophomore	senior	junior

17

Chapter 4

First Self-driving Car Trial on Public Roads

I Warm-up Activity

Where would you like to go on a drive?

....

....

写真を説明する英文 (1 sentence) を書いてみましょう。

....

....

II Listening

音声を聴き、写真の説明にもっとも近い英文を選びましょう。

Answer   Ⓐ   Ⓑ   Ⓒ   Ⓓ

Chapter 4

III Check Your Vocabulary 🔊 11

A. 左側の単語にもっとも近い意味をもつ表現を右から選びましょう。

1. trial （　　） a. from far away

2. autonomous （　　） b. to prevent something bad from happening

3. remotely （　　） c. to watch something carefully and record your results

4. monitor （　　） d. a process of testing to find out whether something works effectively and is safe

5. avoid （　　） e. independent and having the power to make your own decisions

B. 左側の定義にあてはまるように、空所を埋めてみましょう。

1. 科学技術 （te ＿＿＿＿ logy ）

2. 歩行者 （pede ＿＿＿＿ an ）

IV Note-taking 🔊 12

本文を聴きながらノートを取りましょう。（英語でも日本語でも構いません）

19

V Dictation

音声を聴き、(　)を埋めましょう。答え合わせをしたら、音読しましょう。

First Self-driving Car Trial on Public Roads

Japan's first self-driving car trial on public roads began today in central Aichi prefecture. The prefecture, a (¹　　　) company and Nagoya university are working (²　　　) to realize level four autonomous driving technology. This enables AI to control the gas pedal, steering, and brakes. In June, the (³　　　) Police Agency ordered that self-driving car tests be remotely monitored. The vehicle aimed to drive about 700 meters going 15 kilometers per hour, while avoiding traffic and pedestrians. Officials hope to make self-driving cars a (⁴　　　) by 2020, in line with the government's (⁵　　　).

http://www.ntv.co.jp/englishnews/society/first_self-driving_car_trial_on_public_roads/

Score	/ 5

VI Comprehension Check

以下の文章を読んで、内容が正しければT、間違っていればFに○をつけなさい。

1. Self-driving car tests have been conducted on public streets for many years.　(T ／ F)

2. AI is used to control the self-driving cars.　(T ／ F)

VII Write/Speak about Yourself

Would you like to ride in a self-driving car? Why/Why not?

VIII Vocabulary Building

下の選択肢から英訳を選び、表を完成させましょう。

自動車の部分に関する英単語（米語）	

日本語	英　語
フロントガラス	1 （ ）
ハンドル	2 （ ）
サイドブレーキ	3 （ ）
日よけ	4 （ ）
運転席	5 （ ）
助手席	6 （ ）
クラクション	7 （ ）
バックミラー	8 （ ）
サイドミラー	9 （ ）
ウィンカー	10 （ ）

driver's seat	horn	side-view mirror	blinker	steering wheel
hand brake	sun visor	windshield	passenger seat	rear-view mirror

Chapter 5
Japan Mulls Congestion Pricing for Kyoto, Kamakura

I Warm-up Activity

What tourist spots would you like to visit in Japan?

写真を説明する英文（1 sentence）を書いてみましょう。

II Listening

音声を聴き、写真の説明にもっとも近い英文を選びましょう。

Answer ▶ Ⓐ Ⓑ Ⓒ Ⓓ

III Check Your Vocabulary　🔊 14

A. 左側の単語にもっとも近い意味をもつ表現を右から選びましょう。

1. charge 　　 (　　) 　　 a. the problem of too much traffic in a place

2. congestion (　　) 　　 b. to make a vehicle stop or move more slowly

3. toll 　　　 (　　) 　　 c. relating to the government of a town or city

4. brake 　　 (　　) 　　 d. money that you pay to use a bridge or road

5. municipal (　　) 　　 e. to ask someone to pay an amount of money

B. 左側の英語の意味を日本語で表現しましょう。

1. traffic jam 　　 (　　　　　　　　　　　　　　　　　　　　　　　)

2. ancient capital (　　　　　　　　　　　　　　　　　　　　　　　)

IV Note-taking　🔊 15

本文を聴きながらノートを取りましょう。（英語でも日本語でも構いません）

23

V Dictation

音声を聴き、（　）を埋めましょう。答え合わせをしたら、音読しましょう。

Japan Mulls Congestion Pricing for Kyoto, Kamakura

Japan is considering charging cars to ease traffic at popular tourist sites. The move comes as both tourists and locals (¹   ) of traffic jams. Transport officials are planning a study of congestion pricing for the heavily visited ancient capitals, Kamakura and Kyoto. The (²   ) is to begin from this fall and tolls won't be collected at first. Japan's electronic toll collection system will be used to map popular routes and points where (³   ) brake. The data will show where and (⁴   ) traffic jams happen (⁵   ). Transport officials and local municipalities will use the data to study how to collect tolls.

http://www.ntv.co.jp/englishnews/society/japan_mulls_congestion_pricing_for_kyoto_kamakura/

Score	/ 5

VI Comprehension Check

以下の文章を読んで、内容が正しければT，間違っていればFに○をつけなさい。

1. Drivers are being asked to drive more slowly in Kyoto and Kamakura.　　　　　(T ／ F)

2. Tourists and local people in Kyoto and Kamakura are unhappy with the number of cars there.　　　　　(T ／ F)

VII Write/Speak about Yourself

Which season do you think is the best for sightseeing in Japan? Why?

VIII Vocabulary Building

空欄を埋めましょう。

お金に関する英語

Across→

2. 暗証番号
4. 銀行
5. 利子
6. 現金
7. 借金
9. 手数料

Down↓

1. サイン、署名
3. 罰金
5. 収入
8. 税金

Chapter 6

All Aboard the 'Love Train'

I Warm-up Activity

How do you come to school?

写真を説明する英文（1 sentence）を書いてみましょう。

II Listening

音声を聴き、写真の説明にもっとも近い英文を選びましょう。

Answer ▸ Ⓐ Ⓑ Ⓒ Ⓓ

Chapter 6

III Check Your Vocabulary 🔊 17

A. 左側の単語にもっとも近い意味をもつ表現を右から選びましょう。

1. operate　　（　　）　　a. full of something

2. replete　　（　　）　　b. the words you say to a god

3. prayer　　（　　）　　c. to use and control a machine

4. unsuspecting（　　）　　d. to regularly travel between work and home

5. commute　　（　　）　　e. not knowing that something bad is happening

B. [　] 内の文字を並べ替えて、左側の日本語と同意の英単語にしてみましょう。

1. 性分・精神　s[i i p r]t　　（　　　　　　　　　　　　　　　　　）

2. 公開する　　u[e i n v]l　　（　　　　　　　　　　　　　　　　　）

IV Note-taking 🔊 18

本文を聴きながらノートを取りましょう。（英語でも日本語でも構いません）

V Dictation 🔊 18

音声を聴き、（　）を埋めましょう。答え合わせをしたら、音読しましょう。

All Aboard the 'Love Train'

Valentine's Day is no longer just a (¹   ) day for people—a train in Tokyo is getting into the (²   ) spirit. Keihin Kyuko Line, a (³   ) railroad that operates in and around Tokyo, today unveiled a special Valentine train. The Keikyu 'Love Train' is replete with hearts inside and out. Even the straps in the cars are heart-shaped. What's more, a Shinto priest conducted a special prayer over the straps. So unsuspecting (⁴   ) best beware that Cupid could strike them silly with love when they least expect it—such as when they're commuting into work. The train will run until (⁵   ) 14.

http://www.ntv.co.jp/englishnews/society/all_aboard_the_love_train/Score

Score	/ 5

VI Comprehension Check

以下の文章を読んで、内容が正しければT，間違っていればFに○をつけなさい。

1. The Valentine train can be seen across Japan.　　　　　　　　(T ／ F)

2. A Shinto priest created the heart-shaped straps.　　　　　　　(T ／ F)

VII Write/Speak about Yourself

What is the most special day for you?

VIII Vocabulary Building

下の選択肢から英訳を選び、表を完成させましょう。

形に関する英単語	

日本語	英　語
正方形	1 （　　　　　　　　　　　　　　　　　）
丸	2 （　　　　　　　　　　　　　　　　　）
三角形	3 （　　　　　　　　　　　　　　　　　）
長方形	4 （　　　　　　　　　　　　　　　　　）
五角形	5 （　　　　　　　　　　　　　　　　　）
六角形	6 （　　　　　　　　　　　　　　　　　）
星　形	7 （　　　　　　　　　　　　　　　　　）
楕　円	8 （　　　　　　　　　　　　　　　　　）
立方体	9 （　　　　　　　　　　　　　　　　　）
球	10 （　　　　　　　　　　　　　　　　）
円　柱	11 （　　　　　　　　　　　　　　　　）

star-shaped	triangle	oval	rectangle	pentagon	cylinder
circle	cube	hexagon	sphere	square	

Chapter 7

Seven Eleven Japan to Add Lockers for E-commerce

I Warm-up Activity

How often do you go to a convenience store? Which services do you use?

....

....

写真を説明する英文 (1 sentence) を書いてみましょう。

....

....

II Listening

音声を聴き、写真の説明にもっとも近い英文を選びましょう。

Answer   A   B   C D

III Check Your Vocabulary 🔊 20

A. 左側の単語にもっとも近い意味をもつ表現を右から選びましょう。

1. customer（　　　）　　a. something difficult you are responsible for

2. deliver　（　　　）　　b. to take goods or letters to a particular place

3. burden　（　　　）　　c. to try very hard to do something difficult

4. struggle（　　　）　　d. someone who buys goods or services from a shop

5. shortage（　　　）　　e. a situation in which there is not enough of something

B. [　] 内の指示に従って、単語を書きかえましょう。

1. convenience　［形容詞形に］　（　　　　　　　　　　　　　　　　　）

2. keep　　　　　［過去形に］　（　　　　　　　　　　　　　　　　　）

IV Note-taking 🔊 21

本文を聴きながらノートを取りましょう。（英語でも日本語でも構いません）

V Dictation

音声を聴き、（　）を埋めましょう。答え合わせをしたら、音読しましょう。

Seven Eleven Japan to Add Lockers for E-commerce

Japan's convenience store chain Seven Eleven will add lockers in its stores where customers can pick up packages delivered by Yamato Transport. The service will begin at 30 stores in Tokyo starting in (¹   ). Seven Eleven will keep the packages in these lockers for 3 days. E-commerce has been rapidly growing in Japan and that's become a burden on Yamato Transport. The (²   ) goes door-to-door to hand packages, but when their customers are not (³   ), the firm has to go back to redeliver. As a (⁴   ), many drivers have been working longer (⁵   ). Other convenience stores like FamilyMart and Lawson have also started setting up lockers as well.

http://www.ntv.co.jp/englishnews/society/seven_eleven_japan_to_add_lockers_for_e-commerce/

Score	/ 5

VI Comprehension Check

以下の文章を読んで、内容が正しければT，間違っていればFに○をつけなさい。

1. Thanks to growing e-commerce in Japan, many drivers work shorter hours.　　（ T ／ F ）

2. Seven Eleven is the only convenience store chain in Japan with lockers in its stores.　　（ T ／ F ）

VII Write/Speak about Yourself

Which do you prefer, going to shops or shopping online? Why?

VIII Vocabulary Building

下の選択肢から英訳を選び、表を完成させましょう。

Phrasal Verbs	Definition
go back	1　(　　　　　　　　　　　　　　　　　)
set up	2　(　　　　　　　　　　　　　　　　　)
put up with	3　(　　　　　　　　　　　　　　　　　)
come across	4　(　　　　　　　　　　　　　　　　　)
give in	5　(　　　　　　　　　　　　　　　　　)
hang out	6　(　　　　　　　　　　　　　　　　　)
work out	7　(　　　　　　　　　　　　　　　　　)
cut in	8　(　　　　　　　　　　　　　　　　　)
find out	9　(　　　　　　　　　　　　　　　　　)
hang up	10　(　　　　　　　　　　　　　　　　)

to surrender	to spend time with someone	to exercise
to meet or find by chance	to interrupt to discover	to tolerate
to end a phone call	to return to a place to arrange	

Chapter 8
Kumamoto Castle Repaired in Symbol of Quake Restoration

I Warm-up Activity

Have you ever visited a castle?

写真を説明する英文 (1 sentence) を書いてみましょう。

II Listening

音声を聴き、写真の説明にもっとも近い英文を選びましょう。

Answer   Ⓐ   Ⓑ   Ⓒ   Ⓓ

Chapter 8

III Check Your Vocabulary 🔊 23

A. 左側の単語にもっとも近い意味をもつ表現を右から選びましょう。

1. noted   (   )   a. to decorate something

2. sculpture (   )   b. imagined or invented

3. mythical   (   )   c. well known or famous

4. adorn   (   )   d. continuing for only a limited period of time

5. temporary (   )   e. an object made out of stone or wood by an artist

B. [ ] 内の文字を並べ替えて、左側の日本語と同意の英単語にしてみましょう。

1. 地震   e[a a h k q r t u]e   (   )

2. 建造物   s[c r r t t u u]e   (   )

IV Note-taking 🔊 24

本文を聴きながらノートを取りましょう。（英語でも日本語でも構いません）

35

V Dictation

音声を聴き、(　)を埋めましょう。答え合わせをしたら、音読しましょう。

Kumamoto Castle Repaired in Symbol of Quake Restoration

Two years since a series of earthquakes damaged a castle in southwest Japan, rebuilding is making (¹　　). Two huge quakes struck Kumamoto City killing 264. The famous Kumamoto Castle was heavily damaged. It lost its noted symbols—sculptures of a mythical carp that adorn the tower. Last (²　　) a brand-new 100 kilo sculpture was placed atop the east side of the repaired tower. For the (³　　) of Kumamoto who can see it from all over it's a big boost to their spirits. Later this month another carp will be placed on the (⁴　　) side. With the castle's repair things are looking up. But on the other side of town thousands remain stuck in temporary (⁵　　).

http://www.ntv.co.jp/englishnews/society/kumamoto_castle_repaired_in_symbol_of_quake_restoration/

Score	/ 5

VI Comprehension Check

以下の文章を読んで、内容が正しければＴ、間違っていればＦに○をつけなさい。

1. The castle was seriously damaged by the quake.　　　　　　　　(T / F)

2. A brand-new carp was placed on the west side.　　　　　　　　(T / F)

VII Write/Speak about Yourself

What is your hometown famous for?

VIII Vocabulary Building

空欄を埋めましょう。

Irregular Verbs		
V1 Base Form	V2 Past Simple	V3 Past Participle
1 ( )	lost	lost
2 ( )	brought	brought
mistake	3 ( )	4 ( )
come	5 ( )	come
break	6 ( )	7 ( )
8 ( )	caught	caught
choose	9 ( )	10 ( )
11 ( )	12 ( )	stuck
13 ( )	14 ( )	struck

Chapter 9

Training to Bike

I Warm-up Activity

What are the advantages of cycling instead of driving?

....

....

写真を説明する英文 (1 sentence) を書いてみましょう。

....

....

II Listening

🔊 25

音声を聴き、写真の説明にもっとも近い英文を選びましょう。

Answer   Ⓐ   Ⓑ   Ⓒ   Ⓓ

III Check Your Vocabulary ◄)) 26

A. 左側の単語にもっとも近い意味をもつ表現を右から選びましょう。

1. sneak peak （　　） a. a brief showing

2. disassemble （　　） b. without difficulties and worries

3. fold （　　） c. to separate something into its different parts

4. hassle-free （　　） d. to make something smaller by closing it

5. peninsula （　　） e. a long, thin piece of land that has water around most of it

B. [ ] 内の指示に従って、単語を書きかえましょう。

1. enthusiast ［形容詞形に］ （　　　　　　　　　　　　　　　　　　　　　　　　　　　　）

2. scenic ［名詞形に］ （　　　　　　　　　　　　　　　　　　　　　　　　　　　　）

IV Note-taking ◄)) 27

本文を聴きながらノートを取りましょう。（英語でも日本語でも構いません）

V Dictation

音声を聴き、（　）を埋めましょう。答え合わせをしたら、音読しましょう。

Training to Bike

A new (¹   ) for bicycle and travel enthusiasts is just around the corner. East Japan Railway gave the media a sneak peek at a new train this morning. The Boso Bicycle Base has been (²   ) for bicycle lovers who want to get out of the concrete jungle of Tokyo for some scenic cycling. (³   ) train passengers have to disassemble or fold their bikes and bag them before taking them on trains. This new mode of transport will allow them to strap them up hassle-free. It will transport cycling enthusiasts between (⁴   ) Tokyo and Chiba Prefecture's Boso Peninsula, which makes up the eastern edge of Tokyo Bay. The service will start operating on (⁵   ) 6.

http://www.ntv.co.jp/englishnews/society/training_to_bike/

Score　　／5

VI Comprehension Check

以下の文章を読んで、内容が正しければT、間違っていればFに○をつけなさい。

1. Cyclists will be able to get around Tokyo easier with this new service.　　(T ／ F)

2. Passengers normally have to make their bikes smaller to carry them on trains.　(T ／ F)

Chapter 9

VII Write/Speak about Yourself

Would you prefer to live in a downtown area or in the countryside?

VIII Vocabulary Building

空欄を埋めましょう。

鉄道関係の英語

Across→

1. 切符
5. 遅延
6. 駅のホーム
8. 発車

Down↓

2. 車掌
3. 通路
4. 通勤する
7. 時刻表

41

Chapter 10

Robot Phone Rentals to Start

I Warm-up Activity

What places would you recommend to foreign tourists visiting your town or city?

....

....

写真を説明する英文（1 sentence）を書いてみましょう。

....

....

II Listening 🔊 28

音声を聴き、写真の説明にもっとも近い英文を選びましょう。

Answer　　Ⓐ　Ⓑ　Ⓒ　Ⓓ

Chapter 10

III Check Your Vocabulary 🔊 29

A. 左側の単語にもっとも近い意味をもつ表現を右から選びましょう。

1. available　(　　)　　a.　at the beginning

2. device　　(　　)　　b.　to buy something

3. purchase　(　　)　　c.　a machine or tool that does a special job

4. convey　　(　　)　　d.　to communicate or express something

5. initially　(　　)　　e.　able to be used or can easily be bought

B. 左側の定義にあてはまるように、空所を埋めてみましょう。

1. 製造業者　　(manufac ＿＿＿ er)

2. 目的地　　　(d ＿＿＿＿ ination)

IV Note-taking 🔊 30

本文を聴きながらノートを取りましょう。（英語でも日本語でも構いません）

43

V Dictation

音声を聴き、（　）を埋めましょう。答え合わせをしたら、音読しましょう。

Robot Phone Rentals to Start

Visitors to Tokyo will soon be able to add a taste of sci-fi to their (¹   ) by renting a robot smartphone. Starting April 25, Robophone will be available for rent. The device can engage users in English or Chinese and goes for 1,500 yen or about $13 per (²   ) hours. Until now the device was only available for purchase and in Japanese. Billed as the world's first robot smartphone, the Robophone is made by electronics manufacturer Sharp. Robophone is targeting (³   ) visitors and uses a global positioning system to determine its location and convey relevant information to users. Rental locations and area coverage are to be expanded. Initially rentals will be limited to Haneda Airport and the device will (⁴   ) information for just a few major (⁵   ) destinations.

http://www.ntv.co.jp/englishnews/world/robot_phone_rentals_to_start/

Score	/ 5

VI Comprehension Check

以下の文章を読んで、内容が正しければT，間違っていればFに○をつけなさい。

1. Robophone is now available for rental in Japanese.　　　　　　　　(T ／ F)

2. Sales of Robophone started April 25.　　　　　　　　　　　　　　(T ／ F)

Chapter 10

VII Write/Speak about Yourself

What kind of things would you like a robot to do for you?

VIII Vocabulary Building

空欄を埋めましょう。

国籍の英語

日本語	英　語
アメリカ人	American
イタリア人	1 （ ）
オランダ人	2 （ ）
カナダ人	3 （ ）
スイス人	4 （ ）
ドイツ人	5 （ ）
フランス人	6 （ ）
ニュージーランド人	7 （ ）
オーストラリア人	8 （ ）
ベトナム人	9 （ ）
タイ人	10 （ ）

45

Chapter 11

Record Minors Fall Victim to Crimes through Social Media

I Warm-up Activity

How often do you use social media?

....

....

写真を説明する英文 (1 sentence) を書いてみましょう。

....

....

....

II Listening

 31

音声を聴き、写真の説明にもっとも近い英文を選びましょう。

Answer   Ⓐ   Ⓑ   Ⓒ   Ⓓ

Chapter 11

III Check Your Vocabulary 🔊 32

A. 左側の単語にもっとも近い意味をもつ表現を右から選びましょう。

1. minor   (   )   a. to have a bad effect on something

2. victim   (   )   b. someone who is thought to be guilty of a crime

3. embroil (   )   c. someone who has been attacked, robbed, or murdered

4. harm   (   )   d. to be involved in a difficult situation

5. suspect (   )   e. someone who is below the age at which they become legally responsible for their actions

B. [ ] 内の指示に従って、単語を書きかえましょう。

1. underage ［日本語に］   (   )

2. kind   ［名詞形に］   (   )

IV Note-taking 🔊 33

本文を聴きながらノートを取りましょう。（英語でも日本語でも構いません）

V Dictation

音声を聴き、（　）を埋めましょう。答え合わせをしたら、音読しましょう。

Record Minors Fall Victim to Crimes through Social Media

A (¹   ) number of Japanese minors fell victim to crimes through social media in 2017. The National (²   ) Agency says 1813 minors were victimized via social media last year. That's the highest since record keeping began in 2008. But the number of minors victimized through online dating websites declined. Twenty-nine were embroiled in crimes this way last year. Of all the underage victims harmed via social media, (³   ) pornography accounted for 570, or one-third. That's up six-fold over the past (⁴   ) years. In terms of service providers 695 child victims used Twitter, a three-fold increase over the last two years and the largest of all platforms. When asked why they met the suspect, 23 percent of victims responded, citing "the suspect's kindness" and "willingness to listen to their (⁵   )."

http://www.ntv.co.jp/englishnews/society/record_minors_fall_victim_to_crimes_through_social_media/

Score	/ 5

VI Comprehension Check

以下の文章を読んで、内容が正しければT，間違っていればFに○をつけなさい。

1. More and more Japanese minors are becoming victims of crime through online dating websites. (T ／ F)

2. Crimes related to Twitter have decreased dramatically. (T ／ F)

Chapter 11

VII Write/Speak about Yourself

Do you think we need to be careful when using social media? Why or why not?

VIII Vocabulary Building

下の選択肢から英訳を選び、表を完成させましょう。

法律・犯罪に関する英単語	

日本語	英　語
逮捕する	1 （　　　　　　　　　　　　　　　　　　　）
脅迫する	2 （　　　　　　　　　　　　　　　　　　　）
虐待	3 （　　　　　　　　　　　　　　　　　　　）
中毒	4 （　　　　　　　　　　　　　　　　　　　）
共犯者	5 （　　　　　　　　　　　　　　　　　　　）
犠牲者	6 （　　　　　　　　　　　　　　　　　　　）
裁判所	7 （　　　　　　　　　　　　　　　　　　　）
逃亡者	8 （　　　　　　　　　　　　　　　　　　　）
有罪	9 （　　　　　　　　　　　　　　　　　　　）
窃盗	10 （　　　　　　　　　　　　　　　　　　）

theft	fugitive	victim	accomplice	addict
arrest	guilty	abuse	court	blackmail

Chapter 12

New App Aims to Cut Food Waste

I Warm-up Activity

Do you often go to the supermarket to buy a lot of food?

写真を説明する英文（1 sentence）を書いてみましょう。

II Listening

音声を聴き、写真の説明にもっとも近い英文を選びましょう。

Answer Ⓐ Ⓑ Ⓒ Ⓓ

Chapter 12

III Check Your Vocabulary 🔊 35

A. 左側の単語にもっとも近い意味をもつ表現を右から選びましょう。

1. trial （　　）   a. to cut

2. reduce （　　）   b. to take a photograph

3. snap （　　）   c. to throw something away

4. discard （　　）   d. a person or shop that sells goods to the public

5. retailer （　　）   e. a test to find out whether something works effectively

B. 左側の定義にあてはまるように、空所を埋めてみましょう。

1. 同等の　　（ e ＿ ＿ ＿ valent ）

2. 期限切れ　（ e ＿ ＿ ＿ ration ）

IV Note-taking 🔊 36

本文を聴きながらノートを取りましょう。（英語でも日本語でも構いません）

51

V Dictation 🔊 36

音声を聴き、（　）を埋めましょう。答え合わせをしたら、音読しましょう。

New App Aims to Cut Food Waste

A new app in Japan aims to cut food waste. Nippon TV's reporter has the story. Trials to reduce food waste with the new app "eco buy" kicked off today in Tokyo. The (¹   ) and cell provider, NTT docomo (²   ) the test. If customers buy food close to the best-by or expiry dates, they get points. When customers use the app to snap a (³   ) or label, they get points equal to 20 percent of the (⁴   ). In Japan, about 30 percent of food is discarded. Retailers try to fight waste by adding discount labels on products nearing expiration. But facing a labor shortage, retailers find it (⁵   ) consuming. Store owners hope the new app proves successful in encouraging consumers to buy food close to expiry in exchange for points.

http://www.ntv.co.jp/englishnews/economy/new_app_aims_to_cut_food_waste/

Score	/ 5

VI Comprehension Check

以下の文章を読んで、内容が正しければT、間違っていればFに○をつけなさい。

1. A new app gives users discounts for buying food close to its expiration date.　（ T ／ F ）

2. It is very easy for shop owners to add discount labels.　（ T ／ F ）

Chapter 12

VII Write/Speak about Yourself

What attracts you to buy something at a particular store?

VIII Vocabulary Building

下の選択肢から英訳を選び、表を完成させましょう。

Phrasal Verbs	Definition
kick off	1 ( )
blow up	2 ( )
check out	3 ( )
get along	4 ( )
turn down	5 ( )
look after	6 ( )
run over	7 ( )
take off	8 ( )
black out	9 ( )
let down	10 ( )

to start	to rehearse	to faint	to refuse
to like each other	to take care of	to disappoint	to explode
to pay one's bill and leave a hotel		to start to fly	

53

Chapter 13

Japan High School Girls Least Happy with Body Shape: Survey

I Warm-up Activity

How many times a day do you look in the mirror?

....

....

写真を説明する英文 (1 sentence) を書いてみましょう。

....

....

II Listening　　　🔊 37

音声を聴き、写真の説明にもっとも近い英文を選びましょう。

Answer ▶   Ⓐ   Ⓑ   Ⓒ Ⓓ

Chapter 13

III Check Your Vocabulary 🔊 38

A. 左側の単語にもっとも近い意味をもつ表現を右から選びましょう。

1. figure （   ）   a. worried

2. respondent（   ）   b. angry or annoyed

3. irritated （   ）   c. the shape of the human body

4. cooperate （   ）   d. to work together for a particular purpose

5. concerned （   ）   e. a person who answers a request for information

B. ［ ］内の指示に従って、単語を書きかえましょう。

1. satisfied ［名詞形に］   （   ）

2. positive ［反対語に］   （   ）

IV Note-taking 🔊 39

本文を聴きながらノートを取りましょう。（英語でも日本語でも構いません）

55

V Dictation

🔊 39

音声を聴き、（　）を埋めましょう。答え合わせをしたら、音読しましょう。

Japan High School Girls Least Happy with Body Shape: Survey

Japanese girls are the least satisfied with their figures. That's according

to a survey of high school students in Japan, the U.S., China and South

Korea by Japan's National Institution for Youth Education. The wide-

ranging (^{1}　　　　) survey found US respondents with the highest

percent who said they are "somewhat irritated on a (^{2}　　　)

basis" at 69.7 percent. China had the highest rate of high schoolers who

said they cooperate well with others at 89.5 percent. Japanese high

school students had the highest rate of actual normal weight among the

four countries. But the majority of (^{3}　　　　) respondents lacked a

positive body image. Just 23 percent of Japanese girls said they were

satisfied or (^{4}　　　　) satisfied with their body shape. The head of the

institute said Japanese students are too concerned with others' opinions.

He said he hopes students will find something good about (^{5}　　　　).

---

http://www.ntv.co.jp/englishnews/society/japan_high_school_girls_least_happy_with_body_shape_survey

Score	/ 5

VI Comprehension Check

以下の文章を読んで、内容が正しければT，間違っていればFに○をつけなさい。

1. The majority of high school students in China say they can work with other people. (T ／ F)

2. Less than a quarter of Japanese high school students are worried about their looks. (T ／ F)

Chapter 13

VII Write/Speak about Yourself

What were you interested in most during your school days?

VIII Vocabulary Building

左の国名の首都を探しましょう。（たて・よこ・ななめ）

首都の英語

Country's names

China

Indonesia

Thailand

Egypt

Canada

South Korea

Malaysia

Spain

France

Italy

E	C	G	O	A	O	U	T	R	A	E
B	E	I	J	I	N	G	W	P	O	L
N	J	B	P	O	O	M	R	U	R	L
K	U	A	L	A	L	U	M	P	U	R
I	U	N	K	I	R	R	D	O	A	R
S	O	G	E	A	U	I	E	E	I	O
U	E	K	W	I	R	S	S	P	R	M
A	R	O	K	D	I	T	R	I	A	E
U	E	K	A	O	T	T	A	W	A	M
L	I	M	L	K	K	C	N	I	A	K
U	I	R	A	E	D	P	R	T	U	R

BEIJING	JAKARTA	PARIS	CAIRO
OTTAWA	SEOUL	KUALA LUMPUR	
MADRID	BANGKOK	ROME	

57

Chapter 14
Chiba Likely to Make 'Geologic' History

I Warm-up Activity

Are you interested in ancient history?

写真を説明する英文 (1 sentence) を書いてみましょう。

II Listening

音声を聴き、写真の説明にもっとも近い英文を選びましょう。

Answer   Ⓐ Ⓑ Ⓒ Ⓓ

Chapter 14

III Check Your Vocabulary   🔊 41

A. 左側の単語にもっとも近い意味をもつ表現を右から選びましょう。

1. dub   (   )   a. layers of rock or earth

2. strata   (   )   b. a period of time in history

3. garner   (   )   c. to collect information or support

4. hurdle   (   )   d. to give someone or something a funny name

5. era   (   )   e. a problem that you have to deal with

B. 左側の英語の意味を日本語で表現しましょう。

1. apply to   (   )

2. magnetic pole   (   )

IV Note-taking   🔊 42

本文を聴きながらノートを取りましょう。（英語でも日本語でも構いません）

V Dictation

音声を聴き、（　）を埋めましょう。答え合わせをしたら、音読しましょう。

Chiba Likely to Make 'Geologic' History

Chibanian. It may sound like the (¹   ) of a character from a Japanese anime or game app. But Chibanian is looking increasingly like a word that will one day be included in school (²   ). Japanese researchers applied to the International Union of Geological Sciences to have a new geologic age dubbed Chibanian, named for an ancient strata along a river in a cliff in Ichihara, Chiba Prefecture. Sources say that Chibanian garnered about 60 percent (³   ) in the (⁴   ) round competing against other candidates. It would refer to the geologic age from about 770,000 to 126,000 years ago and indicate the last time that the north and south magnetic poles switched. While there are still a few more hurdles to be (⁵   ), it is quite possible that next year Chibanian could become the first geologic era named after a location in Japan.

http://www.ntv.co.jp/englishnews/society/chiba_likely_to_make_geologic_history/

Score	/ 5

VI Comprehension Check

以下の文章を読んで、内容が正しければT、間違っていればFに〇をつけなさい。

1. Chibanian is named after a character in a Japanese anime.　　　　（ T ／ F ）

2. The name Chibanian is easily recognized as a new geologic era.　　（ T ／ F ）

VII Write/Speak about Yourself

If you could go back in time, what period would you visit?

VIII Vocabulary Building

下の選択肢から英訳を選び、表を完成させましょう。

地学に関する英単語	

日本語	英　語
地質時代	1 （　　　　　　　　　　　　　　　　　　　）
風化作用	2 （　　　　　　　　　　　　　　　　　　　）
浸食作用	3 （　　　　　　　　　　　　　　　　　　　）
活断層	4 （　　　　　　　　　　　　　　　　　　　）
溶岩	5 （　　　　　　　　　　　　　　　　　　　）
化石燃料	6 （　　　　　　　　　　　　　　　　　　　）
震度	7 （　　　　　　　　　　　　　　　　　　　）

weathering   active fault   seismic intensity   fossil fuel
geological age   erosion   lava

Chapter 15
Japan May Be Allowed to Boost Tuna Catch

I Warm-up Activity

What's your favorite kind of sushi?

....

....

写真を説明する英文 (1 sentence) を書いてみましょう。

....

....

II Listening

 43

音声を聴き、写真の説明にもっとも近い英文を選びましょう。

Answer Ⓐ Ⓑ Ⓒ Ⓓ

Chapter 15

III Check Your Vocabulary 🔊 44

A. 左側の単語にもっとも近い意味をもつ表現を右から選びましょう。

1. rebound ( )   a. determined to do something

2. likelihood ( )   b. to increase or improve something

3. negotiate ( )   c. the chance that something will happen

4. tenaciously ( )   d. to have a formal discussion with someone

5. boost ( )   e. to increase again after decreasing

B. 左側の英語の意味を日本語で表現しましょう。

1. bluefin tuna   (   )

2. Fisheries Agency   (   )

IV Note-taking 🔊 45

本文を聴きながらノートを取りましょう。（英語でも日本語でも構いません）

63

V Dictation 45

音声を聴き、（　）を埋めましょう。答え合わせをしたら、音読しましょう。

Japan May Be Allowed to Boost Tuna Catch

The (¹　　　　) of pacific bluefin tuna may be headed down. New research shows stocks rebounding. That means Japan and other countries may be allowed to boost catches. If it seems likely stocks will rebound to a (²　　　　) level by 2024, an international (³　　　　) says catches can be raised. Japan's Fisheries Agency says the body monitoring bluefin stocks released results this (⁴　　　　) showing an increased likelihood stocks will rebound. Fisheries Minister Ken Saito said he would negotiate tenaciously to boost Japan's catch. But the country broke its limit for small bluefin last year and is already near its limit for this year. In focus is how far Japan can push for a (⁵　　　　) catch.

http://www.ntv.co.jp/englishnews/world/japan_may_be_allowed_to_boost_tuna_catch/

Score	/ 5

VI Comprehension Check

以下の文章を読んで、内容が正しければＴ，間違っていればＦに○をつけなさい。

1. The number of bluefin tuna seems to be increasing.　　　　　　　　（ T ／ F ）

2. Japan will have to try hard to get permission to catch more bluefin tuna.　（ T ／ F ）

Chapter 15

VII　Write/Speak about Yourself

Name a dish typically eaten in your area. Explain how it is prepared.

VIII　Vocabulary Building

空欄を埋めましょう。

魚貝類の英単語

Across→

3. サケ
5. カニ
6. クジラ
7. タコ

Down↓

1. ウナギ
2. カツオ
3. サメ
4. コイ
8. マグロ
9. イワシ

65

Shadowing/Reading Aloud Record Sheet

Chapter	1st time		2nd time		3rd time	
	Shadowing	R/Aloud	Shadowing	R/Aloud	Shadowing	R/Aloud
1						
2						
3						
4						
5						
6						
7						
8						
9						
10						
11						
12						
13						
14						
15						

日付を記入しましょう。

Dictation Sheet

Dictation Sheet

Dictation Sheet

MEMO

MEMO

【著者紹介】

津田晶子 (Dr. Akiko TSUDA)
専門分野：TESOL、異文化間教育。通訳案内士（英語）

金志佳代子 (Kayoko KINSHI)
専門分野：英語学（日英対照研究）、英語教育

Kelly MacDonald
専門分野：翻訳、英文校正

Copyright ⒸＣ日本テレビ放送網株式会社

NTV News24 English 2
日テレ News24 English で考える日本事情 2

2019年1月15日　初　版

津　田　晶　子
著　　者ⒸＣ金　志　佳　代　子
Kelly MacDonald

発　行　者　佐　々　木　　元

発　行　所　株式会社　英　　宝　　社
〒101-0032 東京都千代田区岩本町2-7-7
Tel. [03] (5833) 5870　Fax. [03] (5833) 5872

ISBN 978-4-269-17024-7 C1082
［製版:㈱マナ・コムレード／印刷:㈱マル・ビ／表紙:伊谷企画／製本:井上製本所］

本テキストの一部または全部を、コピー、スキャン、デジタル化等での
無断複写・複製は、著作権法上での例外を除き禁じられています。
本テキストを代行業者等の第三者に依頼してのスキャンやデジタル化は、
たとえ個人や家庭内での利用であっても著作権侵害となり、著作権法上
一切認められておりません。